Praise for Len Verwey's *In a Language That You Know*

"Contemplative and lyrical. . . . 'When I cannot find you / I give your name to everything.' Such poems employ the periphery as an active, sometimes disquieting space from which to imagine. Such poems disarm me into sorrow, into hope."
—Aracelis Girmay, author of *The Black Maria*

"Poems in this book plunge you, without warning, from a mattress on the floor, a village bus stop, or a fisherman's boat into the depth of human aloneness. . . . Len Verwey writes: 'You need to breathe / in stone, breathe out a flower.' He accomplishes this mission in his book: breathing in history and landscape, he breathes out powerful, fervent lyricism."
—Valzhyna Mort, author of *Collected Body*

"A quiet exploration of life in a country tinged with violence, social inequality, and dark history. The poetry, however, is never overtly political or judgmental. Verwey's touch is much lighter, mostly drawing on personal experience to highlight the problems of a male culture that applauds machismo and sexual conquest. . . . Verwey's poetry is characterized by precise language and an intense lyricism that speaks directly to the heart of the reader. . . . Despite the dark uncertainty, there's also a sense of precarious hope."
—Alison Flett, *Transnational Literature*

LOVING THE DYING

African
POETRY
BOOK SERIES

Series editor: Kwame Dawes

LOVING
THE DYING

Len Verwey

University of Nebraska Press / Lincoln

The African Poetry Book Series is operated by the African
Poetry Book Fund. The APBF was established in 2012 with
initial support from philanthropists Laura and Robert
F. X. Sillerman. The founding director of the African
Poetry Book Fund is Kwame Dawes, Holmes University
Professor and Glenna Luschei Editor of *Prairie Schooner*.

Library of Congress Cataloging-in-Publication Data
Names: Verwey, Len, author.
Title: Loving the dying / Len Verwey.
Other titles: Loving the dying (Compilation)
Description: Lincoln : University of Nebraska Press,
[2023] | Series: African poetry book series
Identifiers: LCCN 2023010378
ISBN 9781496234681 (paperback)
ISBN 9781496238337 (epub)
ISBN 9781496238344 (pdf)
Subjects: LCSH: Death—Poetry. | BISAC: POETRY /
African | POETRY / Subjects & Themes /
Death, Grief, Loss | LCGFT: Poetry.
Classification: LCC PR9369.4.V49 L68 2023 |
DDC 821/.92—dc23/eng/20230303
LC record available at https://lccn.loc.gov/2023010378

Set in Garamond Premier by L. Welch.
Designed by N. Putens.

CONTENTS

LOVING THE DYING

I Lit a Fire

Your sort of place, they'd said,
looking back as they left.

Winter ocean, shuttered houses.

I stood on the white sand
under the hawking dark
and I was laughing,
or I sang my finished song for guitar and knife.

Sometimes I forgot the words for things
but never for that song.

A wispy girl with her dog would
stop and talk to me
every thousand years,
still craving love as I craved love.

In the afternoon onshore
loosened beams in every structure
beating against each other without cease.

I lit a fire out among the dunes
then extinguished it.

Only a monster or a ghost could care
for you, they'd said.

I said I know.

As I walked I blinked my eyes,
not sure what else was needed.

They'd return soon, they'd said,
but they didn't.

As I knew they wouldn't.

Homecoming

I let everyone know I'd be home soon,
and they believed me,
then I waited for too long.

Mothers and fathers, brothers and sisters:
they prepared my rooms again
though they shouldn't have.

All that love does was done to me
but I wasn't much of a son.

Look how thin I am,
look how quiet I've become
I want to say.

I'd like to think I'm without desires now
but I know that's not true.

The strange boy that I was, long ago,
softly let me go
when I raged to be let go of.

Perhaps he should've held on.

I'd have a quick talk with him now.
A quick talk, mind, neither of us can bear
sentimentality.

Anyway, though I won't be coming home
I have other places to go.

I don't regret anything, but I'd like to tell him
everything that's happened.

The Mind Has a Phone of Its Own

The mind has a phone of its own,
punches away in the dark.
It wants to know, and know immediately:
what ground is holy, what water drinkable,
what teaching can be trusted and which
stranger to give a place to stay.
What to steal and what
to buy and what to give away.
It grows tired, but will not give in,
will not descend into the orchard
from the branch
where it perches and calls,
though the wind picks up fiercely.
It doesn't know who to call
under the black unreceiving sky.
There must be, it thinks,
chimes in a distant muddy arena,
chiming just for me alone,
sounding my special way home,
celebrations just for me, and just out of hearing.
But it may not be so.
How it holds itself in the storm
before the storm of its utter failure.
As though, unanswered, it could never fall
into the wilder wonder of all,
just beyond the dull silence
and the dull doubts it knows.

A Boy Like You

A boy like you must be cunning
until the saving facts are found.

Scrounger city, waif city.
Backs of restaurants, gang corners.
The underways and sundrains and charnel trains,
walking and walking and always
walking, the canal that flows
from any spot all the way to a summer Spain.

Or so they say.

Maybe you'll write a song one day, become famous.
For now, because you know
all the unknown places, you make yourself useful
to the scoundrels' and the tricksters' work.

Turn away fiercely from the offered hand
of the kind man
on the bicycle beside the highway.

Better to pretend to believe,
for as long as it suits you,
the well-dressed old man in the bookshop,
who fakes a shared interest
in the book of maps you pick up.

You are not interested in maps either.
Take his gold watch when he's asleep.

A city is a hard kiss, an opened arm in a suite.
A gray verse and a red chorus.
But the lame ordinary people,
thinking it is peace time,
trust a boy like you, open-faced, foolishly.

At home your father said
Now I am almost dead
what do you want to say to me?

But you keep quiet.

Your employers pay in money, things,
new words, always on time.

Meanwhile the corruptible police begin searching
for a boy like you, who pretends
to have no father, who
can sometimes not stop talking, who makes
his room pretty with
what he steals from others' rooms.

Who writes in code even when
he doesn't need to.

If they found you
who knows what they'd do
but they don't know where to look.

Water

I was afraid of the deep side of the swimming pool
in the caravan park just this side of Mozambique.

My father was gone, missing, living without a trace
in Lourenço Marques as the war concluded there,

and I was here in a dusted dry caravan park
with my mother and my little brother.

The pool had been the promise that lured
me away from him, the Old Spice man in the suit with the pipe.

You can swim every day, you'd love that, my mother said,
wouldn't you? But because it turned out to be deeper

than she'd thought, and because I was afraid anyway,
I was only allowed to hunker in the shallow end,

water to waist level, hapless toad boy,
while she sat on a picnic blanket nursing my brother.

I didn't dare go past the middle line, though I pretended
I was accommodating her whims and fears.

I was terrified of the deep end and I was terrified
of other children arriving, seeing me in my cowardly state,

the mark of something on me, making fun of me,
maybe in a language I knew,

maybe in one I wouldn't understand, for though
I was South African I had never really lived here,

not until now, but luckily it wasn't the season
for caravan parks, it wasn't holidays, it was almost empty,

very quiet, no other children, we were there
not because we were on holiday

but because my dad was across the border where we couldn't be,
and this was the closest we could get to him,

and my mother walked to the pay phone with us
in the morning and evening

and spoke to her mother and her sister, but not to my dad,
who was in a city where the phones were dead

and the army was in the street, he was working in the embassy,
he was skeleton staff, my mother said, but I didn't know

what that meant, sometimes she cried, and I wondered
would he bring presents when he arrived back.

It didn't sound like there'd be presents,
if there weren't even phones.

I Was Fifteen

I was fifteen.
Once a week, sometimes more,
I'd walk the four kilometers
to the music shop in Bad Godesberg,
to stare at the guitars in their window.
It was 1988, I'd decided I was without a country,
and I was too shy to go into the shop.
I was afraid I wouldn't know what to say
if the man asked what I wanted, once I was inside.
What did I want?
I was inventing a new country, but how to say that?
Someone might laugh.
There were guitars, without a doubt, in my country,
but standing in the street looking
was enough for me, for now.
Sometimes you'd hear an electric being played,
like a lullaby for an insomniac
long-distance missile,
like an elevator shaft turned sideways
calling for help.
What I wanted then is what I want now,
thirty years later.
Nothing has changed, except I have guitars.
I still don't have a country,
though they've let me stay
here without too much fuss.
They can see I'm harmless.

And I am.
I've remained close to the places
from which you go
to the places that seem the same as
your own glowing mind, when it glows.
That would be the full truth.
Better not to say it so.

Guitar

When we arrived in South Africa, 1988,
I had an Ibanez acoustic in a hard case,
and my hair was in my eyes,
and I was practicing the mixolydian
in the bathroom of the hotel where we stayed
two months, waiting for our house,
driving my brother crazy.

Rehearsals: malperforming amps, the inevitable
retarded drummers, the dusty afternoons
and blue-sky Saturdays, walking to the café
to buy and smoke a thousand and one cigarettes
while the neighborhood watched us,
daunted, threatening to call
the noise police but never doing it.
The forces of dark creativity would prevail, we knew.

Back at home I was trying to write songs
with the five chords the band played well.
I knew enough to know
five chords was enough but whether we had
the right five chords I couldn't tell.

And the setbacks were legion, the quotidian
would not be left out.
Waiting months for the bassist to get up to speed,
then the second guitarist broke his finger,

then the singer's 50cc had to get fixed
so he could make it to rehearsals again.
That took forever.

Eventually you're tired and the songs arrive,
and just like that you have a set
and possibly one day a gig.

Meanwhile ignored totally
by the roughly 13 650 girls in our broader area,
who didn't give a damn what we did one way
or another, never did, never would.

Had we written *Layla*
or been able to play, impeccably and at twice
the recommended speed, Giancarlo's last insane piece
for 17-string electrohydraulic guitar
(you build it then you play it),
we still wouldn't have scored with any of them.

There was no more sexless universe
than our suburban universe of song.

I know now that I was thoroughly happy then
but at the time
I knew I was miserable.

Ours

Just keep it for us, we say.

We'll come back to claim
whatever is ours to claim,

another day.
In some versions we drive or even sail away.

Or maybe we wait hours
in the wrong queue,
or you lose the ticket, or I lose the token.

A sense of fearful neighbor faces, grim authorities:
they confiscate all of it,
seeing how we're likely to behave.

Perhaps we are given something perfect
that appears broken, unrecognizable,
in the wrong light
we've chosen.

It may not have our names on it though,
clearly labeled, our names as such,
and so we go astray.

Others may claim it,
mistakenly, dishonestly.

Do we look enthusiastic enough?
As though in some way
it is the first time we are waiting?

Hurry hurry hurry.

Others may be more pushy,
more willing to play rough.

Wave

Our rocky unprotectable island.

The wave from the earthquake
could be at the shore
then in the city before you know it, they said.

Live elsewhere if you can, live wary,
peer over your shoulder
if you choose to stay.

In our dazed perfect unflooded world
things went on as they may.
We were unwary. We did not notice

the people collecting on the roofs,
waving at the sky, later
the garden furniture floating by.

Even the sirens sounded playful to me,
and when the helicopters
couldn't land I chuckled at their strange choreography.

The wave kept going after it hit the shore,
that was all, I thought, and now
the elders cannot care for anything anymore.

In a way it was what we'd been waiting for.
Perhaps if we'd grown thin and strong
like Jesus when he was young, with that

violent human-hearted love for everything,
then perhaps we could've seen ourselves
interfering, strong-shouldered, strong-handed,

getting all the undone jobs done,
unmaking in some ways what the waves had done.
But when she asked how I planned

to save everything and us, and when I asked how
she planned to save everything and us,
we thought that was pretty fun, we pulled

the sodden couch to the window, we said hush, hush.

Deveer

The diplomatic party was still going strong
but I was tired.
I rested in a room upstairs.
The strange assignments, the crisp
articulate gibberish
of my elders had paled; I who so
loved quiet, put out
into a ceaseless babble, year after year,
to wither impeccably in the world.
What I had I didn't want.
I understood more serious problems existed,
but I put the call in to Deveer,
his was the name and number
I'd been given, I didn't know his
real name then and don't know it now,
nor what he looked like, of course, at any rate
he answered after two rings
and without niceties
I said I wanted reassignment, that it couldn't wait,
that there'd perhaps been a misunderstanding
all along, whatever made
them give this work to me,
whatever they might've thought I asked for,
and had in writing from me,
whatever pictures on file and testimonies to the contrary
to draw on, only love and silence
were still interesting, now, to me,
and really always, though I may not

have known it or said it, love and silence
I said again, because of the sound of it,
and not the love of God
and not his silence, the latter
I knew well and as to the former
what might such an eminence know of human love
in its blistered wearisome varieties,
at which point Deveer laughed
appreciatively, as I'd hoped he would, and I said
I want to be young again,
though that isn't quite what I meant,
though I think he knew what I meant,
and I heard guests groan downstairs
and footsteps in a room
above me and a car's red lights
fading into the forest and someone was
crying in a room close by, had always cried,
and a couple perhaps many couples bellowed
in their ecstasies, I mean it was coming on to morning
in the world, there was blood
on my shoes in the graying light, somehow
I'd stayed awake and spoken through the night,
and I asked Deveer
did he remember how I'd walked
hand-in-hand with my father, a Saturday morning,
to the square to watch the hangings and the beatings,
how we children sang for the governor,
all the old songs and some new ones, I said
there's less of it now
without knowing if that was true, but he said
he remembered, he may have been polite,
and later, having not spoken for some time, I asked
Deveer whether he was
still there, and he said he was, yes,

I said honestly I hardly know myself, but softly,
and told him I did not envy him his job,
at which he chuckled; I said pair me
with a dancing bear, code of course,
he said he'd see what he could do, also code,
a formality all of this to him,
though for me the first and only time and so I felt
I needed to say more, I said
beauty isn't the only game around, you know.
He said he knew.
I said anger is unaccommodatable care,
he said you have me there, but anyhow
you did your best.
I could see the room clearly. The dinginess.
The lawn outside. All the silence.
I said freedom ah freedom would be something else again.
By which I meant yes.

The Dead Trees Sing

This must be the road Deveer used
for his trips to the town.
This the stone cottage he paid so much for,
to the amusement of us locals.

It's said some of the people began
calling it Deveer's Road, soon after he arrived,
but the mayor put a stop to it.

I never came up here when he was alive.
Those final years, when he wrote
The dead trees sing
not more not less than before.

He was tired, his biographer writes, the scandal
at W. had affected him more
than even close friends realized.

His health, always indifferent, was failing him.

He wanted a stone cottage,
an occasional trip to the town for provisions,
familiar visitors from time to time.

Here on the porch with its perfect view
of the valley he must've stood
and thought deeply every morning,
as had been his habit all the years.

Apparently one could see him at it,
if the light was right, looking up
from one's apartment
into the clearer air of the ridge.

Like an eagle, a local journalist suggested,
but the editor cut that.

Certainly he was a hero of language
(Deveer, not the editor)
but a complicated, ambiguous legacy nonetheless,
many unconfronted shadows, as the recently
revealed letters to K. suggest.

Later they hated him so much around here,
didn't they, when he was asked
to drive the red bus
at the carnival and declined.

Even the Damage Kid Is Glum

I hear even the Damage Kid is glum,
though he sits at the main table
of the insincere feast.

There were matches everywhere, previously,
unlit matches, boxes and boxes of them.
Now there aren't.

I see his point, though he may exaggerate.
He was in it for the fire,
and the ashy dawns, and the subtle lamentations.

As for me, I miss the cheap shit they were selling
just before the revolution.
It was rubbish but it looked good.

Still, we've done ok.
I'd visit him for old times' sake but we have
our complex different histories,

our old acrimonies.
Maybe I'll wave across the water though,
from my yacht I can barely sail

to his penthouse suite
the guards keep refusing him entry to.

With the Government Official

See the shelters there?
They will not stand a storm, still the people build them
packed together on any slope of land.
That's how it is around here.
What can you do?
Women take hours
shaping clay and sand canals
between the corrugated iron walls
and the driftwood fences,
which the gray-brown torrent,
when it builds again from distance,
will disregard entirely,
to flood again the earth floors and the pathetic
furniture and possessions.
They'll gather around to inspect the damage,
then begin to drain the rooms
and reshape the canals.
See on the angled banks of the stream
the roots of trees protruding.
And though there is all this flooding
the women must still queue
for water at the trickling standpipes
with their jugs and buckets,
empty two-liter plastic bottles,
any receptacle they can find and drag and push
and roll to where they live.
Half or more of the water that's routed here,
from the dam that lies up beside

the mountain pass there,
lost along the way through creaking pipes
and semilegal farm diversions and all
the rusted infrastructure
money is hard to find for these days.
Who's in charge? It depends who you ask.
No one is. The people are.
The government is of course
but I'm the government around here
and I know I'm not.
Maybe the dogs are in charge, you know?
Or the children,
who God knows are everywhere you look.
Sometimes I think all of it's a deliberate obscuring
of simple truths just to annoy me.
I know how egotistical that sounds.
That everything points to something else
that is hidden from me,
and everybody laughing secretly.
That, for example, the children's chalk-ringed games
could be a form of useless code,
as could the graffiti
on every open piece of concrete,
the phone number in the station toilet,
the unread patient records
at the aspirin-for-everything clinic,
surely too (when I start to think like this)
the words of the minister in the clearing
where the mothers gather
for prayer and penance and gossip.
This is neither war
nor the aftermath of war, that ended decades ago,
but it has the same waste and jumble, I suspect,
the same lack of clarity

and endless administrative bungles,
the same mild paranoia.
Sunday afternoon. My Sunday afternoon thoughts.
All would be bearable, today as every day,
if it weren't for the constant singing.

The Duration

The distractible blue-eyed pilot everyone loved
ran after his golden retriever
and the plane took off without him.

Some people had predicted something like this.

Now here we are, ocean, height and emptiness.
No trustable stories from the intercom.

They could say anything, the cockpit lads,
and we couldn't be certain,
but for now whoever's up there is silent.

They're waiting too.

The blue-eyed pilot was never ruffled,
never fazed.
We liked that about him.

A rom-com may start soon, and there's
a rumor the booze will still be free.

I wonder I wonder
could we love each for the duration?

But I already know we can, easily.

The Estate in Shambles, a Melodrama

The estate in shambles, the fundamentals
crumbled, the head bowed and around
the glass the hand and dark outside.

Unread the last note, slipped under the study door.
The creditors on the porch
and the murderous-moded debtors soon to be released.

There won't be mercy
now a shambolic parliament
prevails in the little despot's mind,

now he's ruined the wife the whole town loved
and shipped the children;
with the pale sunrise the jeers from the urchins

and the cripples and the whores, strong
as always in their ragged glee.
Ludicrous the lurching profile, glimpsed

in a shop window, down the cobbles
for bread and cigarettes,
past the square where they used to say

von Stoefenbroek was baptized,
where Deveer was almost executed
but sang for the governor,

beautifully, saving himself and key
members of his entourage, a Saturday morning,
Deveer running through

his repertoire, and the governor weakening,
and father telling of life
in between the plangent songs, clearly

moved, and decades dead now, and the son
enshambled, dimming, cheered
sarcastically on the daily shopping excursus

by the whole gamut of
garden variety residuals
who make up the villagers proper of the village proper,

curve of the old familiar bay, still poignant
in its way, a firstish lover pulling a sheet
over you and her with much

tenderness, unabideable maddening tenderness, apples,
coffee, sand on the feet on a wooden floor
and the bay through the window,

you must've been for a walk to the beach
and returned, happy, surely, long before
the late kingdom, the benighted rule

of Papenwinkel and all that ensued, only Deveer
still alive today of the old familiars,
unbelievably, doing new songs and the old songs still,

almost going from strength to strength,
total utter bore either way, now as then.

Strange Kingdoms

Two years ago, a friend said to me:
get out for a bit, completely out,
go to a town where no one knows you,
where you know no one, don't tell anyone
where you're going, it will do you a world
of good, go as you are, find a place
that is not a holy land for anyone,
that is uncharged with heavy meaning,
a small beach town, say, before or after its boom years,
that doesn't require a passport
but is not overrun by visitors,
rent a room or rooms, you'll need
a bed and a cupboard and a desk and a clean bathroom
and a balcony overlooking what could perhaps
be called a boulevard by the generous in spirit,
become generous in spirit yourself,
some place where you need explain nothing and need not
pretend to know what you do not know,
and have an ice cream every afternoon, that's good,
with a sugar cone, not a regular cone,
and drinks in the evening, and sleep sleep sleep,
especially at first, and go for a swim every day
(choose a coast where the water isn't too cold),
find a more useful sense
of the order of things, whether a true or false sense
hardly matters, wear shorts,
display your thin white legs without shame,
buy a panama hat, acquire strong opinions

about the economy, watch more sports at the corner bar,
sure, you'll not know for the first few weeks
what to do with yourself, the television not working,
no will in you to read, let alone write,
let alone go for a walk, you'll think
a hopeless mistake has been made, you'll hope
someone is tracking you down, that the phone will ring,
that there will be a knock at the door,
even a stranger asking for the Wi-Fi code
at the breakfast table would be something, initially,
even the authorities coming to ask questions
would be interesting, and autumn will arrive,
strange kingdom of shadow and rain
(as someone wrote, insufferably, I forget who),
and twice you'll almost leave, it's only a three-hour drive
to the old life, after all, but I know you
and you won't, you'll stick it out, and after that,
perhaps a week after the last almost-leaving,
and for the first time in a long time
you'll be at your little pine desk early every day,
and leave it hours later, some of the work that is your work
less undone, so that you can walk breezily
down the almost-boulevard,
greet the town fool equably, share a running joke
about the mayor's new car with the veteran
who sells you your cigarettes,
one of which you smoke on a bench
with a view of the ocean,
which will turn out to be too cold to swim in,
at least for you, but never mind that,
you'll think of staying the winter,
and you'll think, ok, so this is joy,
not a strong thing as such, not a state as such,
but what is under the things, under

happiness and unhappiness,
what arrives when you put down
the arrows and the doves and the suit of feathers
and the hat of leather, so to speak,
something almost imperceptible, unforced, unbidden,
and you needn't thank me but you'll also smile and think,
how strange and fantastic that my friend
knew this, and knew what I needed, or suspected
enough of it, two years ago, back in a coffee shop,
mildly hungover just as I was,
a Saturday afternoon, things not really going anywhere,
the friend I haven't seen since then, the city
to which I haven't returned.

The Dead Girlfriends

Driving much too fast, but so what,
they are dead now are they not
and racing against God's own car
with his polished star
on the bonnet, his monogrammed racing gloves
bigger than the planets.

Racing for fun, they think,
nothing at stake, irreverently, as though
it's still just the unbounded summer
of their lives.

Beach road, sand blown across you could
skid and crash on easily
but when you're dead
you're strangely lucky, and you sort of know it.

Though God is gaining ground, incredibly.
This evening stretch of road and coast
must suit his engine and tires well,
and this space that is . . .
what's the word that sounds like lineament
but means in-between, I forget.

Anyway, it must be like a home-game
advantage to him; I told her nothing is final
and once-off only, amazed
at the glory of us and her.

I said incautiously, tomorrow we could do all
of this again,
the wrongest man that ever lived.

Liminal, that's right.

Soon they'll get to the pass.
They could make Riviersonderend before dark,
they'd have to really push it, but knowing them
they have music, knowing them someone
has her bare feet on the dashboard
and someone switches on
the little light above the rear-view mirror
so you hardly see the rushing road.

Knowing them they won't be careful,
racing to meet us
in a room or bar, lucky us, we can wait,
every night they almost make it.

The Sky-Bedazzled, Dark-Bedraggled

—*after the German*

The sky-bedazzled, dark-bedraggled,
water-stricken, mind-usurped

oscillating animal that am I.
That when about to die

does cry cry cry
as though the life held bleakly, resentfully,

ground-befoulingly,
could yet, given one last chance,

in earthly joy abide eternally.

The Large River

She lived close to the banks
of the large river,
the one that empties into the poles
while the living stand where they are,
furious, unfinished, terribly unsafe,
and the water bayed
and the dogs lapped at her heels
but she did not know it, and for long
she was havened, she was ours,
and we could tell ourselves
that we protected her
as we protected each other,
that all protected all in the day and in the night,
that she, like us, was swayed enough
by that, by love, and persuaded enough
by care, to not leave
as she did, the water waving,
having her.

The Girls of All Hours

The girls of all hours
barely notice summer has arrived.

They've heard the seedy stars
explain everything.

Dance by themselves
as though the end were to be seen.

Survivors

We make awkward mincing
movements with our faces and limbs,
but we don't ask questions.

We babble until someone hands us
a silver blanket and a cup.
Some of us remain entirely quiet.

We step farther away from the ripped
fuselage, the derailed carriage,
the crumpled car.

Noise and then silence:
in our remembering it will always
have happened in the dark.

But look:
we are not dead,
our lives are still in our heads,

our hands in each other's hands,
the praying among us
even pray.

In a minute we could look up
to return the gazes
from behind the barrier,

then we could gently wave away
the counselors,
step slowly toward the ambulance.

Fiery sky reflected in the black pools.
The last dust everywhere
falling onto mirrors.

No one knows yet who made it
and who didn't, or those
who do aren't telling.

Trumpet

A man in a gray suit
walks into the woods
with a trumpet in a trumpet case.

Later, music.

How can you love
what appears and disappears?

Like this and like this and like this.

.

As I Still Was

Lacking the goods
I made my way to the smaller towns,
as I'd been urged to.
It took years, I was on foot.
Perhaps I exaggerate.
All around me others were in motion
but often unlike them
in the silent fields
outside the towns I stood motionless.
In a shack in the Karoo, whatever I
could shake at I shook, irked then as always
by the way every nail
remained in place in too many places
I would still walk through, the way no street
caught fire sufficiently in any city that needed burning,
the way things were what they were
regardless is what I mean.
Every life stays in its skin
while a bleakened land enfolds it.
Don't get me wrong, there was also laughter,
but whether it came from
my own throat I can't say.
If someone passed where I stood, I said
I come to you from another country,
lying, though I doubt they cared one way or another.
If you ask what I ate I'll say, regretfully,
people helped me, people were often kind,
Come in, come in

they'd say in their various ways
but I would not, though I took their food.
I think strange stories grew around me then.
Sometimes a quiet over me, almost worth the trekking,
unnamable birds hovering, a blistered moon
until I cried and cried again
and became easy to find.
In many rooms, none of them quite mine,
they asked *What happened to you?*
But why answer.
Possibly they meant well, but we
could hardly mean what we thought
we meant, I could hardly pretend now
that the language we had was adequate,
was hardly going to give it all away
just when the gun in my heart was blossoming,
beautiful unsavable unkillable
as I still was.

Loving the Dying

We tuck them in, place a dry kiss
on a dry brow, rearrange the flowers
and open and close the curtains
(the light is never right for the dying).

At the end of each long shift
we turn up our collars, slink through
the white passages
and quickly past reception and the security guard.

But the dying are cunning.
They peer through our windows,
leave finger smudges on the postbox,
hang clownishly from our rafters.

They sigh from a room next door
we knew to be unoccupied.

Nobody will hold them in their place.

In our back gardens, tired, we ask:
Are there no other jobs, for people like us?
Will we have no other love
but this begrudging, shiftless thing?

The dying chuckle at that,
cozy for the night in the tree houses
we built for our children summers ago.

There are no other jobs and they know it.
There are no safe separated lives.

Loving the dying
is what we have done and what we will do.

On our better days—mornings
almost like the sound of a clarinet,
evenings almost like the sound of a ship's bell—
we know it too.

ACKNOWLEDGMENTS

The following poems were previously published, and I wish to thank the publications for their support of my work:

"As I Still Was" and "I Lit a Fire" (under the title "Place"), in *New Contrast* 46 (Autumn 2018)

"A Boy like You," in *New Contrast* 47 (Summer 2019), under the title "A Boy"

"The Estate in Shambles, a Melodrama" and "Survivors," in *New Contrast* 45 (Autumn 2017)

"Loving the Dying," "Water," and "Wave," in *Transnational Literature* 13 (October 2021)

"Trumpet," as part of the Avbob Poetry Project, 2019, an online initiative

"With the Government Official," in *Botsotso* 16 (2017), under the title "Are the Dogs Perhaps in Charge?"

Eight New-Generation African
Poets: A Chapbook Box Set
Edited by Kwame Dawes
and Chris Abani
(Akashic Books)

New-Generation African Poets:
A Chapbook Box Set (Sita)
Edited by Kwame Dawes
and Chris Abani
(Akashic Books)

New-Generation African Poets:
A Chapbook Box Set (Tatu)
Edited by Kwame Dawes
and Chris Abani
(Akashic Books)

New-Generation African Poets:
A Chapbook Box Set (Saba)
Edited by Kwame Dawes
and Chris Abani
(Akashic Books)

New-Generation African Poets:
A Chapbook Box Set (Nne)
Edited by Kwame Dawes
and Chris Abani
(Akashic Books)

New-Generation African Poets:
A Chapbook Box Set (Nane)
Edited by Kwame Dawes
and Chris Abani
(Akashic Books)

New-Generation African Poets:
A Chapbook Box Set (Tano)
Edited by Kwame Dawes
and Chris Abani
(Akashic Books)

To order or obtain more information on these or other University of
Nebraska Press titles, visit nebraskapress.unl.edu. For more information
about the African Poetry Book Series, visit africanpoetrybf.unl.edu.

Printed in the USA
CPSIA information can be obtained
at www.ICGtesting.com
LVHW041149151223
766480LV00002B/265